THE NORTH DEVON COAST

A shortish guide

Robert Hesketh

Bossiney Books

Some other Bossiney books you may find useful

GUIDES
Devon Beach and Cove Guide
Devon's Geology: an Introduction
Exmoor, a Shortish Guide
Lynton and Lynmouth, a Shortish Guide

WALKS BOOKS
Really Short Walks in North Devon (3-5km)
Shortish Walks in North Devon (5-8km)
North Devon Pub Walks (8-13km)
Shortish Walks on Exmoor (6-9km)
Exmoor Pub Walks (8-13km)

GENERAL BACKGROUND
Devon Smugglers – the truth behind the fiction
Devon Place Names
Devon's History
Devon's Railways
Devonshire Cookbook
Ghosts of North Devon

Whilst every effort has been made to ensure that the information given is correct at the time of going to press, details – especially of venues and facilities – are subject to change beyond the author's or publishers' control.

First published 2011 by Bossiney Books Ltd
33 Queens Drive, Ilkley, LS29 9QW
www.bossineybooks.com
ISBN 978-1-906474-30-0
Acknowledgements
The maps are by Graham Hallowell.
The cover is based on a design by Heards Design Partnership.
All photographs are by the author or from the publishers' own collection.
Printed in Great Britain by R Booth Ltd, Penryn, Cornwall

Sea canoeing and leisure boating, swimming, surfing and sun-bathing, walking and wildlife watching – North Devon's coast is now a major holiday destination

Introduction

North Devon's beautiful and dramatic coast is its greatest, most distinctive asset. It is also remarkably varied, ranging from Hartland's rocky, surf-washed beaches, through the huge sands and dunes of the Taw/Torridge estuary, rich in wildlife, to the surfing beaches of Saunton, Croyde and Woolacombe and the vertiginous cliffs of Exmoor. The whole length is accessible by the Coast Path (170 km on foot), punctuated by road access points and car parks.

Ilfracombe was a historic port which developed as a holiday resort in the 19th century and acquired its appropriately named Landmark Theatre in 1998

North Devon's history

North Devon's history is inextricably bound with the sea. Long isolated from the rest of Britain by poor land communications, North Devonians looked abroad for trade and adventure. During the 16th century Devon emerged as a leading county, second to none in naval defence, overseas discovery and colonisation.

Stephen Burrough of Northam sailed to Russia via the Arctic seas, naming the North Cape in 1553. His brother William became Comptroller of the Queen's Navy and was Sir Francis Drake's Vice Admiral in the famous English attack on Cadiz in 1587, the 'singeing of the King of Spain's beard'. Sir Richard Grenville helped build Bideford's fortunes on trade and plunder. He commanded a fleet of seven ships in 1585, taking his cousin Walter Raleigh to found a colony in Roanoke, Virginia. The colony failed, but Grenville brought home a number of prizes, including a Native American he christened 'Raleigh'.

Bideford was particularly prominent in the lucrative Newfoundland cod fishery, a mainstay of Devon's maritime economy down to the 18th century. Many North Devonians settled in Newfoundland and in New England, as testified by place names such as Barnstable, Mass., Appledore Island, New Hampshire, and Biddeford, Maine.

Barnstaple and Bideford exported Devon ceramics and woollen cloth, importing sugar and tobacco from the Americas – North Devon was second only to London in tobacco. Seventeenth century Bideford gained some fine merchants' houses.

Meanwhile, heavy customs duties, especially on tobacco and spirits, encouraged smuggling. North Devon's skilled seamen were well placed to practise 'Free Trade'. All along the coast they had isolated

J M W Turner's view of goods being landed at Bucks Mills, with Clovelly in the background, in a print dated 1824

beaches and coves to land contraband. In Lundy, well fortified and with only one landing place, they found the perfect smugglers' island. Ships bound for the busy port of Bristol could 'lose' part of their cargo on the way.

Smuggling developed as one of North Devon's chief sources of wealth, until scuppered by drastic cuts in excise taxes in the mid 19th century. Happily, this coincided with the rise of North Devon's new leading industry, tourism. Based on the Romantic taste for wild scenery and the novel fashion for sea bathing, tourism in North Devon was hastened first by improved turnpike roads, later by railways, finally by motor cars.

Barnstaple gained the railway in 1854, Bideford in 1855. Ilfracombe and Lynmouth became popular resorts after the railway arrived in 1874 and 1898 respectively, as their rich heritage of late Victorian architecture shows. However, rival resorts in South Devon had been connected earlier to the burgeoning rail network and drew many more visitors. The imbalance between the more developed and populated south coast and the relatively tranquil North Devon coast still persists.

Despite the North Devon Link Road (dating from 1987) and Barnstaple's bypass and new bridge, driving to and around North Devon still takes time. But why hurry? There's a great deal of beauty and interest all along the North Devon coast, as this guide will show.

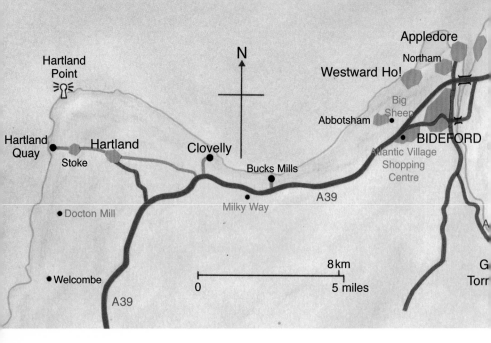

The Hartland Peninsula

Nothing divides Devon's starkly beautiful west-facing Atlantic coast from Newfoundland but the ocean. Salt winds blow almost unceasingly and the restless sea hurls itself against the rocky beaches and high cliffs, fantastically contorted beds of sandstone and shale. Apart from a very few stunted specimens, trees can only survive in the sheltered combes or valleys. Three access points offer parking and opportunities to explore the dramatic but steep Coast Path.

Welcombe Mouth on the Cornish border is the most southerly. A Nature Reserve with high cliffs and a pretty waterfall, it is reached by a narrow lane and then a rough track. Access to the surf-battered beach is by a short, steep path.

Nearby Docton Mill Gardens has a rich succession of native and exotic flowers, including narcissi, primulas, camellias, rhododendrons, azaleas, bluebells and roses. There are special woodland, bog and magnolia gardens at Docton, which prides itself on cream teas.

Hartland Quay is backed by North Devon's most dramatic rock formations. It is more easily accessed than Welcombe, draws more visitors and has a hotel/pub providing refreshments, as well as a seasonal gift shop with a museum above. For the energetic, a 1.25km (3/4 mile) walk south along the Coast Path leads to Devon's largest waterfall at

The beach at Hartland Quay, backed by some extraordinary cliffs

The waterfall at Speke's Mill Mouth, a short walk from Hartland Quay

Speke's Mill Mouth and another dramatic beach of pebbles and saw-toothed rocks.

Despite its exposed position, Hartland Quay once handled a variety of cargoes, notably lime to feed its three kilns and malt for the malt-house. It thrived from Queen Elizabeth's time until damaged by storms in the late nineteenth century.

The museum's maritime exhibits give a vivid impression of the dangers of sailing and trading on this rugged coast, whilst its natural history section explains the area's rich ecology and intriguing geology.

Hartland Abbey

Between the Quay and Hartland village, which has several interesting potteries and galleries, is St Nectan's, Stoke. At 39m (130ft), its tower is the tallest in North Devon and a daymark for ships. Inside are a Norman font and a variety of monuments and brasses, as well as a carved screen, a wonderful ceiling and a small museum

Hartland Abbey

Nearby Hartland Abbey, the family home of the Stucleys, is open to the public. Although elements of the medieval abbey are incorporated into the house, its appearance owes more to the 18th and 19th centuries. There is much of interest, including antique furniture, murals, portraits of prominent local families and archive documents and photographs. It has pleasant sheltered gardens with flowering shrubs, ferns and rare plants. Winding paths designed by Gertrude Jekyll lead down to the sea.

Hartland Point is the third place of access, a short, relatively easy walk from its car park and seasonal café. Looking at the wild seascape, it is easy to understand why the Romans called the Point 'the promontory of Hercules'. It marks the convergence of the Atlantic and Bristol Channel coasts and is a migration area for wild birds; the views south into Cornwall, east along Bideford Bay and north to Lundy are breathtaking. The wind can be equally breathtaking. Despite having had a lighthouse since 1874, the jagged rocks 100 m (330 ft) below remain a serious hazard to shipping, as the now much broken and rusted wreck of *Joanna*, a 970 ton coaster that came to grief in 1982, still testifies. Study the rocks carefully – they are a favourite rendezvous for Atlantic seals.

Seals

Atlantic or grey seals have a British population of around 120,000, mainly concentrated off Scotland but with a sizeable number around Devon and Cornwall. They breed from September to December and the pups are usually born on remote tidal beaches and in sea caves. Mature males grow to over 2 metres and weigh well over 200 kg; the females average a little under 2 metres and a modest 155 kg. Despite their size, seals may be far from obvious (unless they are barking), their grey bellies and black backs merging with the rocks around.

Clovelly harbour. If the prospect of climbing the charming cobbled street does not appeal, there is a regular Land Rover service back to the car park by a back road

Clovelly to Bideford

Along the sweep of Bideford Bay the wind and waves are noticeably less fierce than on the Atlantic coast, but the cliffs are steep and the beaches rocky. Built into cleavages in the cliffs, Clovelly and Bucks Mills enjoy what little shelter this stern coast affords and are the only coastal villages before the sands of Westward Ho! are reached.

Clovelly is exceptionally beautiful and interesting. Preserved by Clovelly Estate as much as possible as it would have been in the mid-19th century, there is nowhere else quite like it. Its narrow cobbled streets are too steep and narrow for cars, which are banned anyway. All goods are transported by hand-drawn sledges, which are parked outside Clovelly's closely packed cottages when not in use. Donkeys no longer carry heavy loads, but children can enjoy rides or visit them at the stables in summer.

Clovelly is centred on its small harbour. The quay is mainly 14th century and many of its buildings centuries old, including the 17th century New Inn and the 18th century Red Lion Hotel. Others were refurbished by Christine Hamlyn, or built under her inspiration and that of the Arts and Crafts movement.

The Hamlyn family had owned Clovelly since 1738. When Christine inherited the estate in 1884, fishing – up till then the village's main source of income – was in decline, but increasing numbers of visitors were coming to admire Clovelly's unique qualities. Christine's policy of banning motor traffic and encouraging donkeys and sledges was both astute and far-sighted. It preserved the Clovelly which Victorian author Charles Kingsley had known and loved and provided funds for its maintenance.

Today's visitors gain a good introduction to Clovelly with a twenty minute film at the Visitor Centre, which also has a café, shops and picnic area. On the walk down to the viewpoint at Mount Pleasant there are workshops – silversmithing, pottery and silk printing, with a range of handcrafted goods, many locally made.

The cobbled street becomes steeper as it descends into the village. Fisherman's Cottage has been preserved with old-fashioned furniture and fittings to show how poor families in Clovelly used to live.

Next door, in the cottage Charles Kingsley often visited, is the Kingsley Museum. Its period photographs of Clovelly are particularly evocative. Tableaux explain Kingsley's love of Clovelly, daily village life, fishing, the lifeboat and the development of tourism.

Take your time to study the house fronts and the side streets on your way down to the harbour, where fishing and sightseeing trips are offered, as well as all-day excursions to Lundy (see page 16).

A ten minute diversion to the right from the old limekiln along Fish Street leads past the Lifeboat station to the rocky beach and to a waterfall.

Clovelly Court Gardens on the way back to the main road makes a pleasing visit. A traditional walled Victorian kitchen garden, it features a wide variety of fruit and vegetables grown in and among flowers. The restored greenhouses with their original fittings are especially interesting.

11

Bucks Mills is comparable to Clovelly, but on a much more modest scale. It shelters in a small, steep valley. Follow signs from Buck's Cross to the free car park, then walk down the lane down to the beach – the last part is steep. There are souvenirs of past industry, a partly ruined quay, disused limekilns and rusting winches. Whilst cargoes are no longer hauled onto the beach (see the illustration on page 5), boat and beach fishing continues in a small way. The beach and its waterfall are especially impressive when the tide is out.

Westward Ho! has been a popular resort since the Victorian boom in seaside holidays. Although no architectural gem, it has amusements, cafés and pubs aplenty and enjoys a splendid position, facing a vast beach of sand and surf. Inspired by and named after Charles Kingsley's swashbuckling North Devon novel *Westward Ho!* (1855), the settlement was begun as late as 1863. Rudyard Kipling's *Stalky and Co.* was based on his schooldays here at the former United Services College.

A great pebble ridge separates Westward Ho! beach from Northam Burrows, 253 hectares of grassy coastal plain, salt marsh and sand dunes, accessible from the car park and visitor centre. The area is rich in a variety of plants and animals, butterflies and birds including skylarks, wheatears and curlew. Local 'potwallopers' graze their horses and sheep here: ball wallopers play golf.

Appledore's maritime history goes back over 1000 years to the defeat of Hubba the Dane by Odun, Earl of Devon, at Bloody Corner – a roadside memorial marks the spot. More history is revealed at the excellent North Devon Maritime Museum, a Georgian house in Odun Road. Exhibits include model boats and displays on boatbuilding and shipboard life. Old Appledore is recalled through photographs and prints.

Its charming narrow streets, mainly dating from its 17th to 19th century heyday as a port for the North America trade, focus on the Quay, which overlooks the beautiful Taw/Torridge estuary. As well as fishing boats, the Lifeboat Station, numerous pleasure craft and the August Regatta, Appledore provides wildlife and fishing trips.

> **Golf**
> The Royal North Devon Golf Club at Northam Burrows is one of the oldest links courses in England. Other attractive courses along the coast include Saunton, Woolacombe, Mortehoe and Ilfracombe.

Above: the beach at Westward Ho!

Right: the front at Appledore

Below right: The narrow back streets of Appledore are a delight to explore. There are galleries and craft shops, and the village has annual arts and book festivals.

It is still a working port with its own shipyard, and is also home to several artists, for whom the lovely local seascapes and North Devon's special clarity of light are particular attractions.

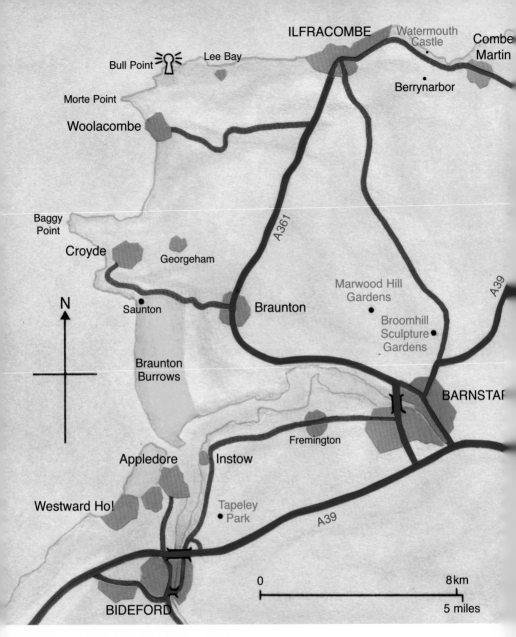

Bideford and Instow

Bideford, like Appledore has a long maritime history, embracing ship-building, fishing and trade with North America. The Burton Art Gallery and Museum in Kingsley Road, located near Charles Kingsley's statue and the 1588 Armada guns in Victoria Park, is a good introduction.

Bideford's Long Bridge was originally built of wood in about 1280 to replace the ford beside which Bideford first developed. It was rebuilt in stone in 1535.

Bideford's Quay, where the Lundy ferry MS *Oldenburg* moors, has been widened and lengthened many times. Bridgeland Street, which runs at right angles to the Quay, is lined with 17th century merchants' houses.

Closer to the Long Bridge, 'The Rose of Torridge' café is essentially a 17th century timber-framed building, probably contemporary with the adjacent King's Arms.

Lundy

Lundy (above) has a remarkably rich flora and fauna, which, along with its isolation from the frenetic modern world, are its greatest attraction. It's a granite island some 5km by 1km, with 120m cliffs. Over 400 bird species have been recorded on the island, including puffins which gave Lundy its Norse name. Seals, dolphins and porpoises are often seen, as are Soay sheep, goats and Lundy ponies. The Warden organises simple outdoor pleasures such as birdwatching, walking, snorkelling, climbing, photography and fishing. See page 32 for how to visit.

Across the Long Bridge in **East-the-Water** the Royal Hotel contains the remains of a 1688 merchant's house. The Allied Chiefs of Staff met in the Kingsley Room in 1944 to plan D-Day.

The lovely *Kathleen and May*, the last wooden-hulled three-masted topsail schooner still sailing in British waters, docks at Brunswick Wharf or Bideford Quay. She was built in 1900 and traded around the British Isles until 1961.

Bideford's railway station operated passenger services from 1872 to 1965. It has preserved buildings, coaches and a small visitor centre (limited opening hours).

The 'Kathleen and May'. Guided tours include the wood-panelled saloon, the cabins and decks, and a shore-based museum

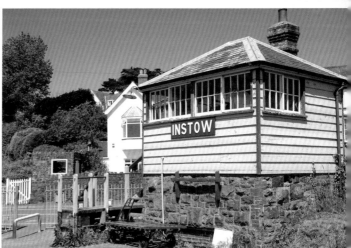

Instow's railway signal box dates from 1872 and is preserved with its levers, a short section of re-laid track and a working signal. It is open on selected Sunday afternoons

Instow's sandy beach is easily accessed and popular with families. Since Instow's development as a Victorian resort the beach has become the focus of the village; old Instow was centred on its parish church. Like many ancient coastal settlements, the village was sited inland, largely out of sight of the sea and Viking raiders. Instow is the HQ of the North Devon Yacht Club – the Taw/Torridge estuary is ideal for sailing. Boat trips and boat hire are available.

Tapeley Park and Gardens
Tapeley Park near Instow enjoys wonderful views over the estuary and on to Lundy. Terraced and walled gardens are complemented by fruit trees and a kitchen garden. Seasonal opening.

Barnstaple seen from the modern road bridge

Barnstaple's Butchers' Row, with the Pannier Market opposite

Barnstaple to Morte Point

The county's best surfing beaches – Saunton, Croyde and Woolacombe – lie between historic Barnstaple, North Devon's largest town, and the jagged rocky headland of Morte Point. Each beach is a sweep of golden sand backed by extensive dunes. Braunton Burrows is the largest, a huge dune system so rich in plant and animal life it was made Britain's first UNESCO Biosphere Reserve.

Barnstaple is the lowest bridging point on the Taw and has been a port and market for over 1000 years. Centred on the 13th century Long Bridge, now supplemented by a 21st century road bridge, the town has many interesting features. Its history can be read in its older buildings (though some are disguised by Georgian and Victorian façades) and its ancient street plan. Boutport Street marks the line of the ditch outside the walls.

Braunton Burrows

When Barnstaple was a busy port in the North America trade its quay was thronged with ships, exporting Devon pottery and cloth and importing tobacco and furs. Queen Anne's Walk was the Merchant's Exchange, but is now the town's Heritage Centre, a themed museum with sights, sounds and animations to give visitors a vivid impression of Barnstaple's history. The Museum of North Devon, in the Square by the bridge, houses collections of archaeology, militaria, natural history and local history. It also contains the Tourist Information Office.

Famed for its award-winning floral displays, Barnstaple has many noteworthy features, including the Norman castle mound, the Guildhall, the Pannier Market and Butchers' Row and the 17th century Horwood and Penrose Almshouses. St Peter's church is famed for its twisted lead spire and nearby St Anne's Chapel was for long the grammar school – its desks are carved with generations of boys' names. John Gay, author of *The Beggar's Opera*, was its most famous pupil.

Braunton's excellent museum has collections showing local trades and agriculture. It holds a huge photographic archive. Maritime history is a speciality. Another display introduces Braunton's Great Field, one of only two surviving extensive medieval strip fields in England.

Innovative multimedia 'Explorers' are available from the adjacent Countryside Centre and from Saunton Sands beach shop. These give three combined audio-visual tours of Braunton. One describes Braunton's history with archive film and interviews; the second Braunton Burrows' natural history; and the third how the Burrows were used for D-Day training in 1944.

Braunton Burrows

Braunton Burrows is one of Britain's largest and most impressive sand dune systems, covering 970 hectares (2328 acres). From spring to early autumn it has a continuous succession of flowering plants, over 600 species including a delightful range of orchids. The Burrows' flora is at its best in June and July.

To visit Braunton Burrows, either use the toll road and the (free) car park at Crow Point or drive along the coast road to Saunton Sands car park. To aid conservation, please use the board walks, or walk on the beach. Whilst the public is generally very welcome on the Burrows, part is used as a military training area. On rare occasions, red flags are flown and this area is closed for live firing. You may see soldiers or military vehicles – keep out of their way and don't touch any debris.

The coast road between Saunton and Croyde has roadside parking so that you can enjoy the magnificent views of Braunton Burrows, the Taw/Torridge estuary and Croyde's famous surfing beach.

Croyde has shops, pubs and tea rooms, and some attractive thatched cottages. There's an easy level walk from the National Trust car park to Baggy Point with excellent coastal views. Colonies of gulls as well as birds of prey and larks, and fascinating formations of shale and sandstone, add to the interest.

Neighbouring **Georgeham** also has vernacular thatched buildings. Henry Williamson (1895-1977) lived in Georgeham between the World Wars and wrote two classics of North Devon's natural history here, *Tarka the Otter* and *Salar the Salmon*.

Broomhill and Marwood Hill Gardens

Marwood Hill Gardens (see photo opposite), 6km north of Barnstaple, are open daily through the year. As well as a great variety of trees and shrubs – some of them rare – Marwood has three lakes and a bog garden. Specialities include rhododendrons, camellias and magnolias.

Nearby Broomhill Sculpture Gardens are clearly signed from the B3230 Barnstaple-Ilfracombe road. They contain more than 300 contemporary sculptures in a rich diversity of styles and media by 60 artists in some 4 hectares (10 acres) of wooded park.

Sun, sand and surf

North Devon's huge sandy beaches are popular with families and surfers alike. Saunton, Croyde, Putsborough, Woolacombe (photo above) and Coombesgate are the leading surfing beaches. Equipment can be bought or hired from the numerous local surf shops and surfing instruction is available too.

On the walk from Mortehoe to Morte Point, with Bull Point lighthouse in the distance

Morte Point to Ilfracombe and Combe Martin

The coastline takes another 90° turn at Morte Point, assuming a more rugged and rocky character east towards Ilfracombe, a busy resort.

The Point itself is reached by a pleasant 1.5 km (1 mile) walk from Mortehoe. There are magnificent views across Morte Bay, with Bideford Bay beyond. The views east are equally impressive, to Rockham Beach and Bull Point lighthouse. Built in 1879, the lighthouse was rebuilt in 1974 following a cliff fall. It has a range of 44 km.

Mortehoe's Heritage Centre provides a cameo of local history. There are interactive games for children and displays about farming, tourism and, above all, shipwrecks. Morte Point's sharp rocks have claimed many ships, including five in the winter of 1852 alone. Not surprisingly, one of Mortehoe's two inns is called the Ship Aground. In the pub garden is the anchor of the SS *Collier*, 114 tons, which ran aground at Rockham Beach in 1914. She was one of the first steamships to carry mail from Australia.

Lee Bay at high tide. When the tide recedes, the coves further east become accessible, with beaches and rock pools to explore

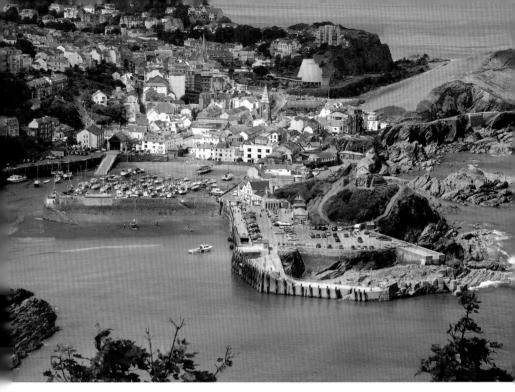

Above: Looking down on Ilfracombe from Hillsborough

Switchback lanes lead to **Lee Bay**, one of North Devon's less frequented bays. Lee has impressive cliffs of folded shale and a delightful inn. Named from creatures of the dolphin family, the Grampus has low beamed ceilings and a pretty beer garden. There is a craft gallery in the Old Schoolroom, further up the lane.

Ilfracombe's superb setting amidst the cliffs helped this important medieval port develop into North Devon's leading Victorian resort. Centred on its beautiful harbour, where fishing boats mingle with yachts and smaller pleasure craft, Ilfracombe is predominantly Victorian in buildings and ambience.

On Lantern Hill above Ilfracombe Harbour there was a beacon fire to guide ships even before St Nicholas Chapel was built there in the 14th century. Secularised at the Reformation, the chapel became a dwelling, but continued as a lighthouse. Now restored, it has a good collection of Victorian photographs and press cuttings, as well as model ships, and provides a lovely view of the harbour – though a more spectacular one is available to those who climb Hillsborough (114m/376ft) to the east of the town.

Ilfracombe harbour, with Lantern Hill and St Nicholas chapel in the background

A variety of boat trips are available from the harbour. The pleasure steamers *Balmoral* and *Waverley* – the last sea-going paddle steamer in the world – offer cruises in the Bristol Channel. MS *Oldenburg* (see page 32) sails regularly to Lundy; a fast ferry service to Swansea is planned for 2011. Wildlife cruises of various lengths combine sight-seeing with opportunities to see birds, seals and dolphins. Charter boats offer fishing trips, but fishing from the pier, the harbour wall and the rocks by Capstone Hill (from where porpoises and seals are frequently seen) is also popular.

Ilfracombe's Aquarium in the old lifeboat station houses more than 100 species of fresh and salt water fish. The new lifeboat station is also by the harbour and the lifeboats are on display when not in action.

Ilfracombe's history, along with natural history, paintings, photographs and Victoriana is displayed at the Museum, near the Landmark. An unmistakable building of two huge white concrete cones, the Landmark serves various roles, including Tourist Information Centre and Theatre.

Hele Corn Mill (seasonal opening) is signed from Hele village on the A399. Restored in the 1970s, it is run as a working museum with an attractive tea garden and handicrafts

No one with an interest in the Victorian age and Ilfracombe's development as a resort should miss the Tunnels Beaches, a fascinating slice of social history. Between 1819 and 1823, 200m of tunnels were cut to give access to these secluded beaches. Period photographs and press cuttings show how segregation between the ladies' pools and the men's pool was strictly enforced until 1905. Victorian biologist Phillip Henry Gosse made the Tunnels Beaches and their rich marine life famous, starting a mania for rock-pooling.

Berrynarbor, a short diversion from the A399 just beyond Watermouth Castle, is a quiet and pretty village with a historic church and pub. Ye Olde Globe has stone fireplaces, period settles and exposed beams. In the pretty garden are stocks, capable of holding one villain.

Chambercombe Manor (photo above), said to be one of Devon's most haunted houses, is signed from the coast road (A399) just east of Ilfracombe. Beginning as an early medieval open-hall house, it has been continuously occupied from Tudor times to the present. Each item has its peculiar history, as is explained during the fascinating guided tours, when visitors are introduced to the chequered and sometimes tragic past of Chambercombe and the spirits said to haunt it. Chambercombe also has delightful gardens, woodland walks and tea rooms.

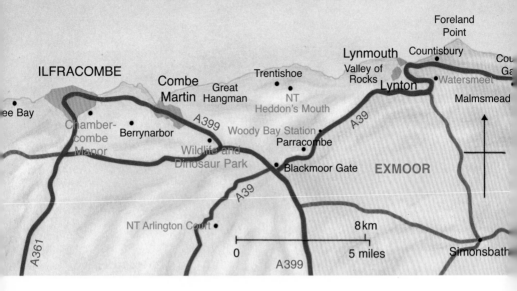

Combe Martin to the Somerset border

Combe Martin marks the boundary of Exmoor National Park and the beginning of the Exmoor coast, which claims the West Country's highest cliffs and one of its most extraordinary geological features, the Valley of Rocks. Lynton, with its cliff railway, waterfalls and deep, rocky gorges was dubbed 'Little Switzerland' – a touch of Victorian hyperbole perhaps, but the scenery is wonderfully dramatic.

Eastwards the moorland meets the sea in a series of dramatically beautiful whale-backed cliffs, rising to over 300m (1000ft) and cut by powerful boulder-strewn rivers and deep gorges. Heddon's Mouth Cleave and Watersmeet have some of the most spectacular scenery in North Devon, rivalled by the Valley of Rocks.

Combe Martin is built into a steep-sided combe or valley. It has one of England's longest high streets leading to a steeply shelving beach surrounded by splendid rock formations. Coastwise trading and fishing, along with silver mining, were Combe Martin's main sources of income from the 14th century until the late 19th and the rise of tourism. More of Combe Martin's history can be discovered in the museum and tourist office by the car park.

For comprehensive descriptions of Exmoor and Lynton/Lynmouth please see *Exmoor: a Shortish Guide* and *Lynton and Lynmouth: a Shortish Guide* in the same series as this book.

The Pack o' Cards at Combe Martin

Half way down the High Street is an extraordinary inn, the Pack o' Cards, which was erected as 'an everlasting monument to Lady Luck' by George Ley, the Squire of Combe Martin, after he won handsomely at cards in 1690. Based on a deck of 52 playing cards, the inn is 52 ft square with four storeys for the four suits. There are 52 windows and 52 steps in the staircase, 13 doors on each floor and 13 fireplaces.

Whilst the hike up to Great Hangman (318 m/1049 ft) is one of the tougher climbs on the Coast Path, the moorland road to Trentishoe gives some fine viewpoints from a series of parking places. The best is obtained by a gentle 500 m walk signed from the parking area up Holdstone Down.

One of Exmoor's most popular short walks starts by the National Trust's shop near Hunter's Inn and leads to the sea at Heddon's Mouth. It's a 3 km (2 mile) fairly level trip on well-surfaced paths. The Cleave (a Devon word for a deep, steep valley) is especially lovely in spring, with wild flowers, and in autumn, for its blazing colours.

The quicker route from Hunter's Inn to Lynton is the A39; the more scenic is the steep and narrow coast road via Woody Bay and Lee Abbey to the Valley of Rocks. The Valley of Rocks may be explored on foot from its car park, or reached by the beautiful, near level and well surfaced North Walk (2 km/1 1/4 miles) from Lynton. North Walk provides marvellous views of Exmoor's high cliffs and on to South Wales.

Woody Bay Station
Part of the Lynton & Barnstaple Railway, Woody Bay Station is restored in Southern Railway style, complete with evocative period paraphernalia. It offers visitors rides (usually steam-hauled) with scenic views to a temporary halt near Parracombe.

The Valley of Rocks. Its unique craggy tors and frost-riven features were possibly the result of glacial action, exceptional in Devon, which lay just south of the ice sheets that covered much of Britain during the last Ice Age. Now a dry valley, it once contained the River Lyn, which left considerable deposits of water-borne rocks.

Another spectacular view, from Lynton's North Walk towards Countisbury Hill

Lynton and Lynmouth are joined by the unique 1890 cliff railway, at the eastern end of North Walk. Gravity-powered by water drawn off the West Lyn, the weight of its two cars is balanced on a pulley system. The top car's tank is filled with water, enabling it to descend whilst pulling up the lighter car with its empty tank 261 m from the bottom of the cliff.

Lynton prospered once it was linked to the main railway network in 1898 and late Victorian architecture, typified by its impressive town hall (now containing the TIC), began to dominate. Housed in an 18th century cottage, Lynton's museum gives a flavour of the smaller, pre-Victorian settlement. As well as a good railway collection, it displays agricultural and craftsmen's tools, period photographs, rocks and fossils, and photographs of the terrible Lynmouth flood of 1952.

The 'Rhenish Tower' in Lynmouth's pretty harbour is a replica of the 19th century water tower destroyed in the 1952 flood.

The valley of the East Lyn, which leads up to Watersmeet

Malmsmead – a tiny village famous for its connection with RD Blackmore's novel 'Lorna Doone'

The 'Rising Sun' is Lynmouth's oldest building. Beginning as fishermen's cottages, it became an inn about 500 years ago and is said to have been used by smugglers, as described in RD Blackmore's Exmoor novel, *Lorna Doone*.

Eastwards from Lynmouth, the A39 climbs to Countisbury. Opposite the 'Blue Ball', a path leads to the church and out towards the Foreland. The views are spectacular. The road continues eastwards towards the Somerset boundary at County Gate: inland, the villages of Malmsmead, Brendon and Rockford are well worth visiting.

Watersmeet
Watersmeet, with its deep wooded gorges and waterfalls, is always impressive. The 3km (2 mile) riverside path from Lynmouth to the National Trust's Watersmeet tea room and information centre is one of Exmoor's finest walks.

The North Devon Maritime Museum at Appledore. The village is also a centre for art and craft galleries

If you enjoy shopping, Bideford's narrow streets harbour a number of small independent shops and places for refreshment

What to do when it rains

Here are some suggested indoor visits – an eclectic mix from theme parks and shopping malls to museums, galleries and historic houses, arranged in west to east order. Some might well provide a whole day out. There are also a number of smaller (but often very good) indoor visits, are described in the main body of the guide.

Milky Way Adventure Park, near Clovelly, offers a range of activities including a huge indoor play area with assault courses and slides, roller coaster rides and live shows.

Atlantic Village is a covered shopping mall on Clovelly Road, which leads from Bideford out to the A39. It includes 35 shops. There are refreshments, a covered play area for children and free parking.

The Big Sheep is a family theme park off the A39 west of Bideford. Sheep shows, sheep racing, horse whispering, the 'Twister' chair-o-planes ride, jumping pillows and live combat zone, etc.

Appledore and neighbouring **Bideford** have plenty to do on a wet day, with museums and galleries as well as inns, cafés and restaurants. If the rain lets up, the quays and old streets are well worth exploring.

Barnstaple's Pannier Market. Barnstaple is the regional shopping centre, and has branches of the large chains as well as a wide range of independents

Arlington Court is a National Trust property halfway between Barnstaple and Combe Martin

Barnstaple has a good museum, a heritage centre and historic buildings as well as many shops and a pannier market.

Ilfracombe – see pages 23-25.

Chambercombe Manor – see page 25.

Watermouth Castle family theme park, 3km east of Hele, has a variety of popular amusements including Gnomeland, Adventureland and Dungeon Labyrinths, a range of refreshments and free parking.

The Wildlife and Dinosaur Park near Combe Martin is set in large grounds. It houses a variety of animals, including wolves, meerkats and sea lions. There are displays and shows, cinema, museum, brass rubbing and The Tomb of the Pharaohs, as well as refreshments.

Arlington Court (National Trust) has tastefully furnished rooms packed with collections of model ships, paintings, seashells, tapestries and pewter. The Victorian stables house an exceptional collection of over fifty carriages and harness. If the weather brightens, there are gardens and vast stretches of parkland to explore. Carriage rides around the estate are offered. Arlington's teas and light lunches are recommended.

Further information

Tourist Information Centres

Barnstaple 01271 375000
Bideford 01237 477676
Braunton 01271 816400
Combe Martin 01271 883319

County Gate 01598 741321
Ilfracombe 01271 863001
Lynton 01598 752225
Woolacombe 01271 870553

Visiting Lundy

Visitors can either go for the day or stay in a range of Landmark Trust accommodation. MS *Oldenburg* sails from either Bideford or Ilfracombe to Lundy between April and October, as well as offering river and coastal cruises; the Hartland Point helicopter flies to Lundy from November to March. Day trips are also available from Clovelly.

Cycling and the Tarka Trail

Traffic-free and mainly level, the Trail is a 51 km (32 mile) long cycle/walkway suitable for short or full day rides for people of all levels of fitness and cycling experience. Starting near Petrockstowe in central Devon, it uses the former railway, incorporating tunnels and bridges. From Bideford, it follows the estuary to Instow and on via Isley Marsh Nature Reserve, Fremington Quay Café and Heritage Centre (a renovated railway station) to Barnstaple and ultimately to Braunton.

Cycles may be hired at several points, including Bideford, Fremington Quay, Barnstaple, Braunton and Torrington.
